Wanderlust

How to
TRAVEL SOLO
Essential tips for independent adventures

Published in 2021 by Welbeck
An imprint of the Welbeck Publishing Group
20 Mortimer Street
London W1T 3JW

Copyright © 2021 Wanderlust Publications
Text written by Lyn Hughes

A CIP catalogue for this book is available from the British Library.

ISBN 978-1-78739-614-2

Printed in China

10 9 8 7 6 5 4 3 2 1

The publishers would like to thank the following sources for their kind permission to reproduce the pictures in this book.

Anna Leskinen/Shutterstock: 4-5, 15, 23, 34, 43, 60, 68, 80, 90, 100, 109, 116

Every effort has been made to acknowledge correctly and contact the source and/or copyright holder of each picture and Welbeck Publishing apologises for any unintentional errors or omissions, which will be corrected in future editions of this book.

Wanderlust

How to

TRAVEL SOLO

Essential tips for independent adventures

WELBECK

Contents

Introduction
6

Chapter 1
WHY DO IT?
8

Chapter 2
PLANNING YOUR TRIP
30

Chapter 3
SLEEPS & EATS
54

Chapter 4
TIPS & TRICKS
76

Chapter 5
DURING YOUR STAY
98

Resources
120

Index
124

Introduction

Let's be clear about solo travel. The fact that you are reading this book means that you are considering or already planning a trip alone... but you are not alone in doing that. There has been a huge growth in recent years in people travelling solo, with travel companies reporting it as one of the biggest trends they are seeing.

And, in case you think that it's not necessarily people like you who are doing it, let's start by busting some common myths:

Myth One. You have to be young. Travel has nothing to do with age – or gender, race or whatever. Whether you are 17 or 70, you can do your first solo trip.

Myth Two. You have to be single. No, not necessarily. It's easy to mix up the words "single" and "solo" but they are not the same – many people who take a solo trip have a partner at home. But there might be practical reasons why they can not always travel together, they may have different interests or they may simply like travelling solo.

Myth Three. You have to be a brave and confident person to do it. There is no doubt that the thought of travelling alone can be scary. But, like overcoming anything that frightens us, it makes us feel so much better when we actually do it.

Solo travel is not about a particular budget or style. There are as many ways to do it as there are if you were travelling with friends or family. Indeed, chances are that you will find things to do that you would have never otherwise considered. Moreover, the sense of freedom it gives you can be quite heady and addictive.

The reasons why we travel are complex and are often misunderstood. It can be a way to reboot and reinvent ourselves, or it can simply be a way to get some headspace, relax and have fun. When planning your trip you may want to consider what you want from it, and we help you do that within these pages.

But the most difficult decision to make is to actually do it, your solo trip. Once you have decided that then the fun bit can start.

So, you have taken the vital first step in buying this book. Now read on, and discover our 100 tips to get you on your way and get the most out of your solo journey.

LYN HUGHES, *WANDERLUST*

Chapter 1
WHY DO IT?

We are perhaps only just beginning to appreciate all the benefits of travel on our wellbeing and of other aspects of our lives.

Most of these benefits are magnified if we travel solo, and indeed there are some that apply only if you travel alone. Indeed, one could argue that the benefits of travel are much deeper and stronger if you do travel as a party of one.

So, whether you have any qualms at all about travelling solo or are just looking for extra justification to take the plunge, read on. You may be surprised at just what your solo trip can do for *you*.

1 *Get to do **what** you want to do*

We're not always aware of how much we compromise in our everyday life. We are eager to fit in with what our friends, family and colleagues want and expect, so a degree of compromise becomes the norm. Doing what we ourselves want to do is considered selfish.

But you may have been on holidays with friends and found that they just want to lie on the beach while you have a yearning to explore the mountains in the distance. Or maybe you have been away with a partner and they want to read a book by a resort pool while you dream of shopping in the souks of Marrakech, taking a tuk-tuk through the streets of Chiang Mai, or riding with gauchos in Argentina.

It could even be you who wants to sit by a pool reading a good book, and you're not getting the opportunity. So, going alone can give you that freedom without feeling guilty for being selfish. You can make the call on where to go and when. You can decide whether to get up pre-dawn to watch the sunrise or whether to snuggle down under the duvet until lunchtime. You can visit as many temples as you want or decide you'd rather chill out in a beachside bar instead.

This is one of the few opportunities in life to do what you want each day.

Building self-confidence

Does the thought of travelling solo terrify you? Don't worry if it does; that's completely normal. Start gently with mini local adventures or take a group tour for at least the start of your trip – see Chapter 2: Planning Your Trip (page 30–53).

But just making the decision to go is a huge step in itself, and once you set the wheels in motion you will probably feel a weight lift off you. Now, imagine when you are back from your solo trip. Just the fact that you actually went through with it will have improved your self-confidence. What's more, the fact that you had only yourself to rely on throughout will have given you confidence. The fact that you wrangled strange transport, menus you didn't understand, unforeseen situations and various niggles will have given you confidence. The fact that you met new people, whether locals or fellow travellers, will have given you confidence. And if things went wrong at any point and you dealt with it… well, that will give you massive self-confidence too. You'll take that confidence home with you as well.

3 *Meet more (and different) people*

We love our circle of friends, but they are very often people who came into our life through circumstance. We met them at school or on the first day of college. They're our neighbours or we work with them. We may have grown and developed in a way that they haven't. Or we may have interests or a world view that they don't completely share.

We may even feel that we know people but have no close friends. Or we may be going through a life change of some sort, whether coming out of a relationship, leaving education, leaving a job, a bereavement or considering a change of career. Some people even start their travelling, their *real* travelling, when they retire.

Travelling solo opens you up to meeting more people. If you're on your own, you are far more approachable than if you're with a friend or in a couple. As a solo stranger you're interesting to people. You'll also find that psychologically you are more interested in meeting people and will be more proactive in making it happen.

What's more, if you're travelling solo, you're more likely to be open to the strangers you meet. You'll come across people confiding things that they would never tell a friend – and you may find yourselves doing the same. It can be very cathartic.

You won't just be confined to your usual "sort" of people either. You'll almost certainly find yourself mixing with a much broader range of people than normal. And if you do have particular interests, then, with a bit of planning, you can find yourself among like-minded people.

4
Self-discovery

Life has a way of hurtling along and we very often don't think too much about who we really are and how we feel about things. About what our values are and what is important to us. This is a chance to really get to know and understand you.

5 *Try on different personas*

In our daily lives we are a reflection of other people and how they see us. Someone's child, sibling, partner, parent. Someone's work colleague, boss, employee. Without realizing it, we fit into a certain role. How would your friends, family or colleagues describe you? You might be the quiet one, the studious one, the over-the-top one, the funny one, the caring one, the sarcastic one. As time goes on, these personas of ours are reinforced and we rarely break out of them.

You might already feel comfortable as you are, but travel can give us a chance to shrug off our personas, experiment and break that mould. The people you meet will have no preconceptions about you, so you are starting with a blank page.

You might find that you have always been the responsible one, and this is the opportunity to let your hair down. People at home may see you as a planner, but now you can be as spontaneous as you like, even leave things to chance. Or have you always been the easy-going one who fits in with everyone else? Now, this is your time.

Trying on a different skin can be disorientating. But it's liberating too, and you'll learn a lot about yourself.

6

Headspace

We lead busy lives in which we are constantly juggling, whether career, education, family, friends, relationships or hobbies. As a result, we rarely have enough time, whether for ourselves or to question the life we are living. We may have emotional baggage to deal with, we may be in a job we don't love, we may be uncertain whether we are on the right path in life.

Stepping outside of the everyday can give you space to think at last. With no pressure or demands, we have the time to consider anything and everything. Of course, you may decide that nothing needs to change when you're back from travel.

But, just having the mental time and space is the opportunity to recharge and reboot.

7 *Live in the moment*

When we're with others, we're in a bubble. Visit any great tourist site, and you will overhear visitors gossiping about someone back home or talking about where they went for dinner last night. They're insulated from the environment they are in and are looking in rather than out. They're thinking about yesterday, last month, tomorrow, next month, instead of thinking about the present.

Travelling solo takes you outside of that. Without the distractions of others, you can give your full attention to what is in front of you. You can focus on the sounds, the smells, the tastes, the colours, the atmosphere. You can truly live in the moment. Savour it.

Flexibility

When there is just you to think about, you can act on a whim, change your plans, be spontaneous.

Want to drop out of the temple tour and head to a café instead? Of course you can! Had an invite to join a hike? Sure, sounds great. Spotted a music performance about to begin? Forget dinner, that looks like it's going to be more fun. Walking past an intriguing doorway? Well, follow your nose and go right in.

You can change your plans, change your accommodation, change your transport, change your clothing, change your mind. We rarely have that degree of flexibility back home and it can be a revelation. It can potentially save you money too as you suss out great deals. It can take you on exciting adventures you wouldn't otherwise have imagined.

9

*Empower yourself to make your **own** decisions*

You may think that you make your own decisions in life, but do you really? How much power do you really have? We may think we make decisions all the time, but do we really? Work decisions may be made with our boss's view in mind. Family decisions are navigated with consideration to the other members.

When you travel solo, your decisions really are down to you, and only you. It starts with the decision that you are going to travel – and travel solo at that. And then it continues through the planning process and onto the trip itself. Being solely responsible for your decisions can be a slightly scary feeling at times, but you will ultimately find it empowering.

10

*Learn to be **comfortable** on your own*

How much time do you currently spend on your own? It might be that you have always lived with people, that you spend your day with work colleagues and have a busy social life or lots of hobbies. Some people are never alone.

If you dread being alone, or find you never quite relax when you are, this could be the time to break that. Returning solo travellers often comment on how the biggest revelation was how comfortable they discovered they felt on their own. They realized that they actually do like their own company.

11 *You can go at your **own pace***

When you've been away and are sightseeing, are you always the last one back onto the bus or into the car? The one who says, "Just one more hour, please"? It's frustrating if you want to wander when your companions want to rush. If you want to sit outside a café people-watching when they can't see the point. If you want to follow your nose up a beckoning street, or when out hiking see what is over the next hill.

Going solo isn't just about where you are going but how you do it and the pace you do it at.

12

*It can **look good** on your CV*

People sometimes worry about the impact that taking an extended break can have on their CV. "Won't it look bad having a gap?" they ask.

Not only are most employers understanding about career breaks, but you can use it to your advantage. What skills did you develop on your trip, whether practical ones (language learning, photography, cooking) or life skills?

Skills to consider mentioning on your CV are:

- Organizational skills
- Budgeting
- Problem-solving
- Decision-making

- Interpersonal skills
- Resilience
- Budgeting

13 *Save **or** splurge?*

Travelling solo means that you can decide not just how much you want to spend but also what on. Whatever your budget, you are in control of it and can decide how to spend it.

You may have been in holiday situations where you wanted to ride in a hot-air balloon at sunrise, but your companion(s) deemed it too expensive and wanted to spend the money on something different. Or maybe you winced at the extortionate dinner bill and wished you could have had the cheap and tasty noodles from a street stall instead. Or did one of you want to take a taxi, while another wanted to walk?

While the stereotypical image of a solo traveller is often of someone on a tight budget, you might be one of the lucky ones who is comfortably well off. You might have found yourself in situations where you felt embarrassed by having more money than friends or family. By going solo, you can book that business class seat, stay in the gorgeous Palace hotel, have a private driver, take a top-class safari.

Whether scrimping or splurging, do hold some of your budget in reserve for unexpected expenses, brilliant opportunities or a well-deserved treat.

14

Savour the quiet

Your life may be noisier than you appreciate. There's the constant intrusion of traffic, technology, people and messages on your phone. At home there might always be music, the radio or television in the background. When was the last time you were conscious of the quiet?

Travelling lets you break from this pattern. You may find yourself listening to nature for the first time in a while. Take time to seek out quiet places. Sit and enjoy a magnificent view. Relish the feelings of your senses. And breathe.

Follow a passion or quest

Do you have an interest that you would love to spend some time immersing yourself in?

Is dance your thing? We met a woman who built her Latin America trip around dance courses. She learned samba in Brazil, tango in Argentina and salsa in Cuba, while practising her moves in numerous clubs in between.

If it's horses that are your passion, then you could ride Andalusians in Spain, Camargue horses in France and Lippizaners in Slovenia. Maybe you have always wanted to go whale watching – this could be your opportunity, not only to try it in one place but to plot your entire trip around whale watching hotspots.

Are you a foodie? There are any number of food or drink trails around the world where you can visit producers and sample their wares. You could do a cookery course or even a whole string of them. We've even met someone who was on a quest to find the perfect *patatas bravas* in Spain.

Or it might be that a member of your family was born overseas, and you have always wondered about their roots. Or perhaps your family lost someone in a far-off land, and this is the chance to track down their grave and pay your respects.

Perhaps a music trail across the United States sounds exciting, or you'd love to follow in the footsteps of your historical hero.

A quest doesn't need to be all-encompassing. But it can, at the very least, add interest and purpose to a journey. Let your imagination run riot.

16

You'll find it more meaningful

Without the distractions of partners, friends or family, you'll find your travel experiences are deeper, more immersive and more intense. You'll be absorbing more, learning more, recording more. Looking back on your travels years later, the experiences that you remember and that affected you most profoundly will be those from your solo trip.

17
Serendipity

By travelling solo, you are opening yourself up to unplanned
events and opportunities. They might not all be amazing, but
go with the flow. Some will be very special indeed.
And some will be serendipitous.

18

*You'll appreciate what you have **back home***

Travel can make you evaluate your life and how you live it. But it will almost certainly make you appreciate aspects back home that you've stopped noticing.

Depending on where you go and what you see, you may find that you have a deeper appreciation of the fact that you are relatively well off financially, that you are educated, and that you have the freedom to roam.

There will also be people that you miss. And you may even find that you are missing unexpected things, such as your favourite radio station, your mum's cauliflower cheese, your morning cappuccino from the little coffee shop you stop in on the way to work. Cherish those feelings.

19 *You'll **grow** as a person*

When travelling you will meet new people, try new experiences, potentially have preconceptions overturned.

You'll learn about yourself and have time to think. You'll almost certainly have to deal with unexpected challenges, small or big. At times, you will step outside of your comfort zone.

You might not even realize at first how travel has changed you, or certainly not all the ways. But it will have had an impact and you will have grown as a person. And the more you travel, the more you will grow.

*You **can change** your life*

It's no surprise that quite a few solo travellers have been inspired to travel when they have either been through a life change or are contemplating one.

As we've seen, solo travel will help you clear your head, give you space and give you confidence.

You'll also be exposed to new people, new experiences and maybe even a new you.

It's not unusual for people who have been on a life-enhancing trip to go home and question their "normal" life. You might find yourself questioning your work-life balance, for instance.

Sometimes the feelings will pass, but you will still feel enriched by your solo travel experience.

Or you could find yourself making far-reaching changes. These could include changing career, taking up a job in travel, moving home, enlarging your social circle or embracing a new hobby.

Travel can be a catalyst for change, and in a positive way. You'll never regret it.

Chapter 2
PLANNING YOUR TRIP

So, you've taken the biggest step – the actual decision to travel solo. This is definitely now going to happen. But, there is the little question of *how* to do it.

Well, with the world as your oyster and so many different ways to travel around it, you may be wondering where to start. There are even more options than you may think, from taking an organized trip to going completely independently to something that combines both.

So, set aside some time to really research and think your trip through. Believe it or not, planning is half the fun.

21 *The **right** trip*

Before you book a flight, ask yourself what you want from the trip. Are you looking to recharge or do you want to be pushed out of your comfort zone? Do you want to follow a hobby or passion, or do you want to have a go at new things? Is it peace and quiet you are looking for or are you happier in a sociable crowd? Do you want to meet new people or are you looking forward to spending time in your own company? Are you more interested in nature or people, cities or countryside, contemporary or traditional culture?

There may not be an answer to these questions, and you may simply be looking for an uncomplicated mix of experiences. However it's completely worth compiling a list of what you do want to do and what you definitely don't.

Now you are ready to think about the destination and how to do it. Solo travel doesn't mean you have to wander lonely as a cloud. There are many ways you can do it, such as going completely independently, joining an organized tour, arranging a private trip or any combination of those elements.

22 *The **right** destination*

Choose a country you'll feel comfortable in for your first solo adventure. For example, you may want to start local by embarking on a trip in your own country; you'll still have a stimulating time, can try different activities to those you would at home, and it will prepare you for an overseas trip.

If you do decide to head overseas, the choice might be dictated by whether you are going independently or not. Maybe start in an English-speaking destination such as Australia, New Zealand, the United States or Canada.

Alternatively, South-East Asian countries such as Thailand, Vietnam and Singapore are popular choices for solo travellers: they offer the right amount of culture shock and unforgettable experiences while the travelling itself is relatively easy. Plus, being so established for tourism, English is widely spoken and understood in the more popular areas. It's a relatively good-value part of the world, so you can make your money go further. You will also meet plenty of other like-minded travellers in these countries.

If visiting a destination you are more uncertain of, consider a group or bespoke tour. And don't forget to check any government travel advisories for the destination.

23

When to go

We could say that there's never a wrong time to go! But do give it some thought. It could, for instance, impact what you should pack. It's also very frustrating to arrive somewhere and find that you should have been there last month. Is there a particular festival you want to witness? If you're into wildlife, when's your best chance of seeing it? If you want a go at surfing, when's best for waves?

Each season in a country will have its pros and cons. Travelling over off season can also mean fewer crowds and lower prices.

24 *Going independently*

You may want to use a specialist travel agent to book your flights. They will, for instance, be able to offer various multi-stop routes or a Round the World ticket – these are typically valid for 12 months. For help with planning your route, it is worth making an appointment with one of their consultants.

Even if travelling independently you may want to book elements of your trip such as airport transfers, internal flights, rail or water legs, and any special excursions. For example, if you will be travelling through Ecuador, and know that you absolutely want to visit the Galápagos Islands, you may want to pre-book that.

Combine group and *independent*

If you like the idea of a big independent trip but are feeling nervous about it, consider joining an organized group tour for the start of your trip, and then taking off on your own after that. For instance, you could join a 10-day tour of Thailand, and then after that carry on travelling on your own through the country and into Malaysia and Singapore.

The organized tour will habituate you to the country or region, and give you confidence before you head off. You will have tuned into the local mores and be feeling so much more comfortable than by diving straight in.

You may find that your guide or tour leader can give you useful tips for your independent travels and that you'll have picked up ideas as you go along. And it may be that some of your fellow travel companions are doing something similar and can become a travel buddy.

26 *Go **group***

Most companies who offer group trips have a good number of solos travelling on them; indeed, it may be that more than half the group are travelling on their own.

While you won't have the same flexibility as you would if you were completely alone, there are several advantages to a group tour. You'll probably get to do more and at a faster pace. You'll be tapping into the expertise of the tour company and guide. You'll have security and backup if anything goes wrong. And companies can sometimes arrange special activities that an individual would find hard to do on their own.

Before booking, feel free to ask the travel company about the make-up of the group you are considering joining – how many couples and singles have signed up? Is it a mixed age group, or are they all a certain age?

27
Share with a stranger

Are you willing to share a room with a member of the
same sex? If so, most travel companies will waive the single
supplement on many group tours. Look out for it as an option
or ask the travel company.

Yes, there's the risk you may be with someone who snores (or
that could be you!), but the tour leader will usually try and do
what they can to help if there are any incompatibilities or
problems. On the plus side, many strangers who share
rooms end up becoming good friends. If there is an odd
number of solo people on the trip, you may be lucky
enough to have a room to yourself without
paying the supplement.

28

*Avoiding the **single** supplement*

Look out for supplement-free holidays; some specialists guarantee it although you may find these are a bit more expensive overall. Others occasionally offer solo-only departures or supplement-free holidays out of season. Some companies may offer a number of supplement-free places on a trip; for example, the first two solo places booked get their own room without paying the supplement.

Alternatively, you may be able to negotiate a waiver of the single supplement when a trip isn't filling. So don't be afraid to ask – just don't expect it during peak season.

Same with hotels and other accommodation. If you can see they are nowhere near full, ask if they will waive the supplement.

 # Challenge yourself

----

Activity and challenge trips, whether trekking, cycling or rafting, tend to attract a high number of solo travellers. They work particularly well because you will build a camaraderie: you're all in it together and (hopefully) supporting each other. Physical effort reduces anxiety and produces endorphins, so you will feel uplifted at the end of each day. Chances are, you'll finish your trip not only having bonded with your tripmates but feeling on top of the world, both physically and mentally.

Is there a charity or good cause that you would like to support? You could go a step further by combining fundraising with a fun trip on a charity trek or cycle ride. A range of specialists offer trips such as climbing Kilimanjaro, trekking to Everest Base Camp or cycling through the Great Wall of China. All attract lots of solos and you'll have the satisfaction of knowing that all your effort has helped others less fortunate than yourself.

30 *Cruising **and** sailing*

We're not just talking huge gin-palace vessels with nightly cabaret acts and multiple restaurants. There are many waterborne options, including expedition cruises, river cruises and a whole range of types of holiday on small boats and yachts.

Expedition cruises explore exciting places like the Arctic and Antarctic. Some of these ships carry fewer than 100 passengers and you all get to know each other. According to Exodus Travels, 35 per cent of travellers on its polar boat trips are journeying alone. Days are spent on excursions whether purely on the water, or by landing somewhere. The only "entertainment" is likely to be expert lectures. You'll have plenty of downtime to relive the day's highlights with your fellow passengers.

And if you're not up for a polar cruise just yet, or want an even more intimate experience, active sailing escapes are great for breaking down barriers, as you're all in it together. Or how about chugging through the canals of the Netherlands by barge, with bicycles available to cycle bits of the towpath when you have the urge?

There are myriad options once you start looking. Relax by island-hopping the Croatia coast on a *gulet*, navigating the Nile by *felucca* or exploring the Kerala backwaters on a converted rice barge. Or how about a flotilla sailing holiday in the Greek islands, where you muck in and have a go? You'll be surprised at the variety available.

31 Safaris and wildlife *trips*

Wildlife-watching trips can be another great option for solo travellers. Days are spent in small vehicles (or on foot) looking for wildlife, resulting in plenty of shared experiences and jaw-dropping moments to discuss over evening sundowners.

Smaller lodges and camps typically have communal seating for meals, but do check this in advance. Swapping tales while sitting around the dinner table or a roaring fire is all part of the experience and will form part of your much-treasured memories. Between activities, you will probably have downtime where you can rest and have some privacy. But equally you'll be able to hang out with your trip-mates.

One warning: do try to get a feel for whether the camp or eco lodge you are interested in is popular with honeymooning couples – you may want to avoid lodges that are overly romantic. But there are plenty who have a high proportion of solos, so just ask if in any doubt.

32

Special interest and learning holidays

Language courses, yoga holidays, cookery, art, photography:
there's an increasingly wide choice of learning trips, and the
majority of other participants will be alone.
Equally, special-interest trips attract like-minded people who
share a hobby or passion. Whether you are into yoga, horse-
riding, cooking or bird-watching, there is almost certainly
a trip for you, and you are practically guaranteed not
to be the only solo. You will have plenty in common
with the other participants and may even find
you make lifelong friends.

Overlanding

These multi-week (or even multi-month) journeys in large trucks typically attract lone rangers. They appeal to travellers with a thirst for adventure, an open mind and an ability to get on well with others – even when living in close confines, 24/7. As they are often lengthy expeditions, overland trips suit solos who – having only their own work and time commitments to worry about – can be more flexible.

However, even solos with limited time can overland: you can often join a trip for just a short leg of the full journey. For example, a truck's entire route might be Tangier to Cape Town (a six-month monster), but you could join the group for a two-week expedition in East Africa. One thing is certain: do a trip like this, and you'll likely make friends for life.

Tailormade travel/ private journeys

If you don't want to join a group of other people, many tour companies and travel agents can tailor a bespoke trip for you, including your own guide and/or driver throughout if appropriate. Alternatively, they can arrange transfers and local guides, where needed. This type of trip can be a good compromise between group and independent travel for those who like some independence and privacy.

With no one else to consider, and no set itinerary to stick to, you can create the trip of your dreams. You are tapping into the tour company's expertise and contacts, and have safety and security, but also as much privacy as you want. Unlike purely independent travel, you also have financial security if anything goes wrong, such as an airline going out of business or travel being disrupted by erupting volcanoes or a pandemic (do check the company is bonded and you have bought a package).

35 *Solo specialists*

There are a number of companies that specialize in tours for solos. On these, 100 per cent of the group will be solos. Trips can range from group stays at beach resorts to house parties in Tuscany to more intrepid exploits.

For example, specialists Solos Holidays offers everything from sun-and-sand weeks in Cyprus to expedition cruises and hikes in the Nepalese Himalayas. On most trips, customers get their own room. Other solo-travel specialists include Just You, Friendship Travel and Travel One.

As with any organized trip you may want to get a feel first for who your fellow companions are likely to be and whether this is the right holiday for you. Feeling the odd one out in a group can be a lonelier experience than being on your own, but with a little bit of research you should be able to find the perfect trip for you.

Volunteering

Volunteering can be a life-changing and fulfilling experience. It comes in many guises, from spending a few days in a dog rescue shelter in Thailand to assisting scientists on a conservation project to two-year VSO projects where you use your skills to help a community.

Just do your homework first and make sure you are going to be doing something genuinely useful and ethical.

Ask the following questions:

- Are you booking through a reputable organization?

- Where does your money go?

- Why do they need volunteers?

- Will what you are doing be genuinely useful longer term?

- Will you be getting training and support?

Get it right, and it could be your best travel experience ever.

37 *Airport lounges*

Splashing out on an airport lounge that you can pay to enter can absolutely be worth it if you have a long time to fill, such as on a layover (you may have to book in advance). Your travel company, airline, bank account or credit card may even offer it as a free perk or at a discount. Otherwise, book it through a provider such as LoungeBuddy, Holiday Extras, Priority Pass or No1 Lounges.

The quality of the lounges and what you get can vary, so do try and research it in advance to see whether it is worth it. But in most you get free snacks and drinks, free (and good) Wi-Fi, plenty of charging points and free newspapers and magazines. It may have shower facilities and even – for an extra cost – spa treatments. Your belongings will be safer than out in the main concourse, the loos will be good and you'll have a comfy seat.

Pack light

There are so many reasons why you should travel as light as possible. You won't have anyone to watch your stuff while you go to the bathroom: therefore, your luggage, or at least your valuables, will need to go with you.

Also, if you are on transport and your luggage has got to go into a hold, then it is out of sight and potentially at risk. So, the ideal is to get your luggage small enough that it can be with you whatever the situation.

Even if that is not possible, think about weight and portability. What if your room is up five flights of stairs and there is no lift – can you carry it up? If you have to walk 20 minutes to your accommodation, can you manage it? There's also the security angle. You'll stand out less and be less vulnerable if you are able to move quickly and easily.

Consider a rucksack so your hands are always free or take a combo of lightweight wheelie and a small backpack for your valuables and essentials.

Don't forget that there are shops everywhere you're likely to go, so pare back and stick to basics. You may want to take old belongings rather than new, so that you can ditch them as you go along if they are no longer needed.

Travelling light not only makes sense, but you will feel much more confident as a result. It's an incredibly liberating sensation.

Pack right

Think layers. Think multi-use. What do you need to take and what can you buy when there? Here's a list of essentials to be adapted as necessary.

- **Jacket or fleece with zip pockets.** What will the temperature be? Will it rain? Will it be cold at night? One good combo can be a lightweight but snuggly fleece that can be a pillow when rolled up, and a super lightweight waterproof shell jacket. Alternatively, a lightweight down jacket that is either waterproof itself, or can be combined with a waterproof on top.

- **Layers**, both short and long-sleeved. Lightweight and either natural (merino wool, cotton, silk) or man-made.

- **Footwear.** One pair of comfortable multipurpose shoes that can take you anywhere from walking a trail to traipsing city cobbles to a restaurant or bar – black trainers are perfect. One pair of sandals, ideally waterproof with a good grip so you can wear them on boats or out walking.

- **Money belt** that goes under your clothes. It should have more than one compartment so you can organize your money and cards and should lie flat.

- **Scarf.** Not only can this make/change your outfit, but it can also be a face mask, head or shoulder covering, pillow, sun protector, wind shield, sling, dust protector, luggage strap... the list goes on and on.

- **Eco-friendly wash** that can clean both you and your clothes.

- **Torch or headlamp**. Indispensable if camping but also useful for power cuts, returning back to base after dark, having to look through something when sharing a room, intimidating anyone who accosts you in the dark.

- **Basic first aid essentials**, including plasters, painkillers, Imodium. Definitely take rehydration salts. Not only will they make you feel a million times better if you get Montezuma's Revenge but they will be your friend when you have a hangover, have exerted yourself on strenuous activity, have got tired and dehydrated, or are just hot and sticky.

- **Basic toiletries and makeup.** Do you need it? Like, *really* need it?

- **Small microfibre towel.** This will be a lifesaver if you do ever need it. And it means you can always go for a wild swim.

- **Hat and sun protection.**

- **Power bank for your phone.**

- **Water bottle** so you don't have to buy bottled water and add to the world's plastic problem.

40 *Take diversions*

There will be times when you are bored, whether on a journey, in a hammock or in your room. Your phone may have everything you need but can strain your eyes. It's good to unplug from technology so think about these instead:

- What about a journal? Capture your adventures or capture your thoughts; this is the perfect opportunity and you won't regret it.

- Colouring book. Not only is colouring fun but it reduces anxiety and generates a feeling of well-being.

- Sketch pad. What do you mean, you can't draw?

  Sketching makes you really observe details, and has been proven to help your brain, your focus and your mental health.

- Pack of playing cards. Not so commonly seen these days, but the advantage of playing cards is that as well as playing by yourself, you can make new acquaintances as they will want to play a game with you.

- A camera. While you can do lots with your phone, your travels could be an opportunity to expand your photography skills. Take a course before you go, or join one when you're away, and then take your camera off automatic and practise. Hopefully, you'll end up with some photos you can hang on your wall at home and you could always produce a photobook to remember your journey by.

- You can take a Kindle or eReader – it is the practical and lightweight solution to reading. But paperback books are even more satisfying and can be used as doorstops, fly swats and window wedges. They can help you meet people too, because you may find yourself striking up conversations with others interested in what you are reading. Yes, they're relatively heavy, but you can always tear out the pages as you make your way through them (ouch!) – though we'd recommend you do a book swap or leave a book where it will be appreciated.

Chapter 3
SLEEPS & EATS

Being in the right accommodation can make or break a trip. And, if you ask people what worries them most about travelling alone, they will often mention their dread of eating alone.

So, while our travel dreams may focus on the wonderful sights and experiences we will encounter, in reality much of our time is actually spent sleeping, eating or thinking about where best to do these.

But fear not, both sleeps and eats can end up as real highlights of your trip.

41 *The **right** place to stay*

When researching where to stay, think about both the type of accommodation you want and where it is situated.

For instance, in a city would you rather be within walking distance of the main sights (which may cost more) or would you be happy being further out and getting around by public transport or taxi? Are some neighbourhoods safer than others? Are there cafés and restaurants nearby? Do you want to be somewhere lively or quiet?

Generally, the hotels to stay clear of are the big, impersonal ones. Small, owner-managed places are often much friendlier and allow for a more sociable experience. Check them out first on a review site to see what people say about the warmth of the welcome and whether they remark on the sociability of the place. You'll find some hosts really do want to go the extra mile to help, and also to introduce guests to each other. Some B&Bs, guesthouses and hotels even have regular social events for guests, such as a daily or weekly happy hour.

Some on-trend hotels now have co-working spaces too, and so may have a programme of networking opportunities and social events. They may be a bit of a hub for digital nomads, in which case you could meet some very interesting and experienced travellers.

42
Home from home

Anything that calls itself a homestay is privately owned, and
it should mean you'll be staying with a family in their home.
However, guesthouses and rentals sometimes brand themselves
as homestays, so make sure you understand what you're booking.
Homestays may be the only option in a remote area, and there are
various schemes around the world to encourage them because
it can help bring low-level tourism into areas off the beaten
track. Wherever you are, you should get a unique insight into
everyday life and a chance to live like a local.
You can also look at Couchsurfing and other hospitality
exchange networks that hook you up with locals,
ensuring you have a friendly welcome
everywhere you go.

43 *Hostel world*

Even if you are not normally a hostel person, consider staying in one. Not only are they good value, but they've come a very long way since the bad old days of single-sex dorms and having to do chores. For instance, check out *The Grand Hostels: Luxury Hostels of the World* by Kash Bhattacharya (aka BudgetTraveller) for some really cool ideas.

Most hostels offer a choice of private rooms or shared dorms, while a few now have individual sleeping pods. Some have bars and include breakfast or offer meals. Many arrange their own activities and events and can book you into tours or help you with itinerary planning. A high number of solos use hostels, and you should find it easy to meet people, although you may still have to make the first move.

Hostels are also a good place to pick up ideas from other travellers – a great waterfall, a restaurant – as well as advice – don't do this tour, do that one, etc.

As with any accommodation, do check first whether it is the right choice for you. Some may have more of a young, party vibe, while others may be *very* quiet. The good news is that there is such a choice of high-quality hostels these days that you'll easily find one for you.

Sleeping in a dorm

If staying in a hostel, you will need to decide whether to sleep in a dormitory or a private room. Your choice will probably be down to budget. If in a dorm, here are a few tips which also apply to any shared accommodation:

- An eye mask and ear plugs may help you get a good night's sleep

- Choose a bed away from the door so you'll be disturbed less

- Check whether the hostel has got lockers or other secure storage for your belongings

- Keep your money belt in bed with you

- Try not to be that annoying roommate who is rustling through their plastic bags at 3 a.m. or who keeps putting a light on

45

Use
communal areas

Try to choose accommodation with communal areas. Sitting in
your room, especially if it's the size of a broom cupboard, can
feel claustrophobic and lonely after a while. So, even if you're
just reading or checking your phone, spend it hanging out in a
nice lobby, lounge or bustling reception area. This may be a
step outside of your comfort zone, but you'll find that when
you're on your own you're much more approachable;
it's a great way to meet new people, to socialize
and enjoy your stay. And people watching is
so much fun!

46 *Affairs of the **heart***

Avoid romantic boltholes! You don't want to be the only solo person staying in a hotel full of smooching honeymooners, no matter how gorgeous it looks in the publicity shots. You could end up feeling lonelier than in a standard hotel. And a rose-petal strewn room is just plain irritating if you're on your own (they stick to you, for a start...). So, if anywhere describes itself as "romantic", book with extreme caution.

47 *Sleeper trains*

Trains are (generally) such an enjoyable way to travel and are the eco-friendly option too. An overnight sleeper train has certain advantages – the ticket may be expensive but you're saving on a night's accommodation. You're not losing a day sightseeing. And rail stations are usually in the city centre, unlike airports for instance. There's also a certain romance to falling asleep to the chugging of a train.

Services and types of sleeping accommodation vary considerably. On some trains, especially in Europe, you can pay extra for a single berth that is lockable. But the majority of services will offer either mixed compartments or seats as the very cheapest option, and the compartments may have doors or not. As ever, do watch your valuables.

Be warned that some of the best services – such as Thailand's service from Bangkok to Chiang Mai – can sell out weeks in advance. So do research your options; we recommend the website seat61.com to get you started.

Motorhome

Want freedom? Love road trips? Enjoy privacy? Then maybe van life is for you.

Campervans have never been more popular, and a growing number of solos are turning to them, especially for travel in Europe, the United States, Australia and New Zealand. Admittedly they are expensive to rent, but you are getting your accommodation included. It's worth having a trial run at home first so you understand the basics, such as connecting electricity and ensuring you have water.

49 *The **right** room*

Perhaps surprisingly, hotels and lodges, especially larger ones, don't always think about the concerns of their solo guests.

What can be particularly galling is to be given a poky room the size of a broom cupboard and with a view over the car park. It's even worse if you have had to pay a single supplement for the privilege. Don't be afraid to ask for a free upgrade to a better room.

Think about your room from a safety and security point of view too. If, for instance, it's a lodge, camping site or complex spread over its own grounds, avoid a room where you have to walk dimly lit paths at night. So, consider whether you would feel happier staying relatively close to reception.

In a multi-floor hotel, the first floor can be the best choice: you won't need to worry about peeping Toms or having your window open, but you will be able to use the staircase if needed – in the case of a fire or other emergency, or if you feel uncomfortable getting the elevator.

Check your room lock works and whether it has deadlocks. If it is opened with an old-fashioned key, don't keep it in the lock. Some travellers like to take a door wedge with them just in case, or to move something in front of the door.

And it might sound obvious, but when leaving your room, double-check it is locked before walking away. Not every room self-locks.

50
Don't order room service

Eating alone, especially in the evening, can be the loneliest part of the solo travel experience. However, don't use that as an excuse to hide in your room – you could be missing out on some great experiences. Take a walk and look for somewhere you will feel comfortable. Or perhaps your hotel can suggest somewhere for you.

*Lunch **munch***

You might feel uncomfortable eating out at night, so if you really don't feel like doing it, make lunch your main meal. One advantage of this is that it is often easier to get a bargain at lunchtime. Look out for set menus and menus of the day – *Menu del Día* in Spanish-speaking countries. In many countries, lunch is still the main meal of the day.

Having eaten at lunchtime takes the pressure off the evening and you can put it to productive use. Maybe book an evening excursion: go to a theatre, concert or cinema. Or use it to do a blog or journal.

Invite people to dine with you

Other solo travellers will be in the same position as you – they need to eat too. So if you see anyone at your accommodation who looks like they might want company, ask if they would like to join you. On a day excursion, you could ask whether anyone is up for meeting later for a meal.

On group tours you are sometimes left to your own devices on the first night in particular, so again see if anyone wants to go out.

Don't just ask other solos either. Couples and friends are sometimes bored hanging out with each other and welcome a new face and new conversation.

Discuss dinner

If you're joining an organized trip of some sort, find out
in advance what happens at dinner. Will you be eating
communally or are evenings free for you to do your own thing?
If you're on a cruise, will it be allocated seating or free seating,
enabling you to vary who you sit with?
The same with safaris; will you be at a table on your own or
are you all sitting together, sharing the highlights of your day?
It can be miserable if everyone else seems to be having a
sociable time but you. The more you know, the more
you can prepare for what's ahead at mealtimes.

Eating right

Take your time to choose the right eating place for you and the mood you are in. As a general rule, avoid quiet and formal restaurants unless you really are in the mood for one. Eating in a café, casual restaurant or a pub can be friendlier and more fun. And check out whether any restaurants have communal tables, which is a bit of a growing trend.

If the staff in the restaurant or bar are friendly (and not too busy), tap into their local knowledge. Visiting the same café or restaurant several times can sometimes be fun as you get to know the staff or owners and they get to know you.

And don't be afraid to strike up a conversation with other solo travellers. Be open and friendly without losing your common sense.

Smile!

Prime position

Don't be intimidated into being seated in a horrible spot at the back of a restaurant or by the toilet. There's no shame in being solo! Choose a nice table where you can people-watch and feel part of the action.

Or, sitting at the counter/bar can be fun, and it gives you the opportunity to talk to the staff as well as fellow customers.

Making time

Rather than dread time alone in your room or in a restaurant, approach it as a positive experience. You can always use the time to write your journal, read a local paper, research, or catch up on social media and your emails. Cherish it and approach it as a positive experience.

57

*Stay **away** from the buffet!*

Upset stomachs are perhaps the most common problem suffered by travellers. All-you-can-eat buffets can be tempting and good value, and many solos are drawn to them as an easy option. But avoid them like the plague; even in a good hotel they can be breeding grounds for germs, the food often being reheated.

You're much better off going to the busy restaurant that the locals are eating at and where the food is freshly cooked. Even a food stall where you can see the dishes being cooked in front of you will generally be a better option.

Street markets and food courts

A great option is to eat at street markets and food courts. You can see the food being cooked, so will know if it's hot and fresh. You can get away with not being able to read a menu too because you can probably see what the food is and simply gesture that you want it. On top of that, they tend to be buzzy and have communal seating, so can be less stressful than eating in some restaurants – and much better value too.

59 *Healthy* *snacks*

Whether you follow a special diet or not, it's a good idea to travel with snacks in case you get hungry while stuck in an empty airport at 3 a.m. or turn up in town when the restaurants are shut.

Dried fruit counts as one of your five a day and doesn't melt in the heat. Look out for Nakd raisins, which are vegan and infused with natural lime, cherry or cola flavours.

However, dried fruit can attract ants even when it's well-wrapped. If you're travelling to the tropics, nuts are an obvious choice – especially as they're packed with protein.

But there are only so many nuts you can eat. Dried seaweed is a good alternative because it's compact, vegetarian and a source of protein, fibre, iodine and vitamin B12. Popcorn is also light to carry. The PROPER brand comes in various flavours, all of which are low-calorie, vegan and gluten-free.

Water filters

If you are travelling to countries with contaminated tap water and want to avoid single-use plastic, invest in a bottle with a filter, which removes bacteria and debris.

Once the bottle is full of tap water, the filter cleans the water – although you'll need to clean the filter regularly.

BRITA's 0.6l fill&go Active bottle is BPA-free and comes with a filter made from coconut shell which removes chlorine. It's squeezable, designed to withstand shocks and has a strap so it's easy to carry or attach to a daypack. Water-to-Go is another brand who use cutting-edge technology to remove viruses, bacteria, chemicals and heavy metals from any non-saltwater source in the world.

Water purifiers remove viruses, too, so if you're travelling to a developing country, it's worth investing in GRAYL's GEOPRESS water purifier. It removes everything from viruses and pesticides to microplastics and heavy metals in eight seconds.

Alternatively, book a trip to Guatemala, where a local invented Ecofiltro, a ceramic pot with a filter that can be found throughout the country.

Make food an experience

Book an eating experience. They are fun ways to get an immersive insight into the local cuisine, get tips and recommendations, and meet fellow travellers. Foodie walking tours are now available in many cities, where you get to visit cafés, bars and shops and sample bits of the local cuisine.

Or for something even more enveloping, sites such as eatwith.com and travelingspoon.com offer supper clubs, dinner parties, cooking classes and other opportunities to eat with locals.

How about a four-course traditional Russian meal in a beautiful St Petersburg apartment, a lively drag queen cooking party in Lisbon, or a seafood feast with a Venetian sailor in an old Italian palace?

You'll also go home with an armoury of new dishes to try out on your friends. And who doesn't love seeing inside other people's homes?

Chapter 4
TIPS & TRICKS

Travelling solo can throw up lots of situations that you wouldn't necessarily face when in company.

There are practical issues to think about such as what to do with your luggage when you go to the loo.

There's also safety. Rest assured that you don't need to be at any more risk if you travel on your own. However, you can certainly feel more vulnerable, and if being harassed or feeling uncomfortable in any way, you will need to have some strategies to overcome the situation.

On *arrival*

You're at your most vulnerable in the first few hours after you've arrived somewhere, and criminals target transport hubs. Avoid arriving at strange airports or stations late at night. If you do have to, then make sure you already have a plan for getting to your accommodation. Get an official taxi from the airport or station or prearrange a transfer. Does your accommodation have a transfer service?

The next day you may be groggy or feel under par due to jet lag, so slow down and give yourself time to make decisions and be extra cautious.

63 *First 24 hours*

Pre-book your first night's accommodation and know how you are getting there. Store the phone numbers and addresses of all accommodation on your phone and on a separate piece of paper.

Before heading out for the first time, ask at reception about any areas that you should avoid. Can you walk everywhere, or should you take taxis? Can you walk around locally at night?

If they have a card with their details on, take that with you when you head out; if there is no card, have it written down on a piece of paper. That way, it will be easy to show to a taxi driver or to a local for directions if needed, and you won't be stuck if your phone battery runs out. If taking public transport, make sure you have a note of the bus routes and stops or train stations.

64

Keep in touch

Always let people know where you're heading, whether your
friends back home and/or the people at your accommodation.
Make sure someone always knows where you are travelling
to next and when you expect to be there. You don't have to
be attached to your phone or calling home every day, but
sharing where you plan to be and when will keep minds
at rest. If heading out with a new friend, make sure
someone knows who you are going with.

65 *Looking* after luggage

Always keep your key valuables on you or close to you, including on a flight. If going to the bathroom, always take them with you.

We're all familiar with the golden rule of never leaving your bag unattended, but with no companion to watch it while you pop to the loo in airports or on public transport, what are you to do?

At the airport, strategically time your toilet break *before* you collect your bag from the carousel. If you do need to nip to the bathroom on a train or bus, try asking someone close to you to keep an eye on it. Make sure you go just *after* a stop to give yourself plenty of time before people will be moving around again.

Wedging your bag into an awkward position on a luggage rack can also deter people from even trying to steal it. Always stow so that zips and fastenings are facing away from people, ideally against a wall.

Whether at an airport or anywhere else, seek out toilets with larger cubicles if you do have to haul your luggage in with you.

Being scammed

It's not uncommon for solo travellers to be targeted for scams, as people assume that they're vulnerable. Polish up your haggling and negotiating skills before you leave and carry yourself with conviction – strong and confident body language can go a long way. Be charming and polite at first to try and diffuse the situation, but if problems continue, walk away and find what you need elsewhere.

If it's a situation that you can't walk away from, such as being charged fake fees, firmly stand your ground and kick up a fuss. You might even have to overreact, but sometimes it really is the only way to avoid being ripped off.

67 *Stay safe*

Keep your wits about you. This means avoiding unlicensed taxis and knowing your alcohol limit, so you stay sober enough to be aware of your surroundings. Remember to watch your drinks, too, to ensure they're not spiked.

Consider investing in a personal attack alarm – and make sure you keep it to hand rather than at the bottom of your luggage. While an alarm won't prevent you from being attacked, it could buy you time by disorientating your assailant and drawing attention to your assault.

The best alarms are easy to activate, tricky to stop and emit a continuous shrill sound over 130 decibels. Practise using one before your trip – just warn your neighbours first.

A good book for safety tips is *The Travel Survival Guide: Get Smart, Stay Safe* by Lloyd Figgins.

68 *Looking after yourself*

With all the excitement of being in a strange destination, and having all of these wonderful new experiences, it can be easy to forget the basics of self-care. If worried you may not be getting a balanced diet, take vitamin tablets.

Keep hydrated, especially in hot countries, at altitude or when doing activities. It's amazingly easy to forget to drink water! Add rehydration salts if you have sweated a lot. Watch what you eat and drink, too. Ice can preserve germs, so have it in your drink only if you have confidence in the establishment. And eat ice cream only from a place you trust.

Avoid touching toilet door handles and any other surface that may harbour germs, unless you can wash your hands immediately afterwards. Always carry anti-bacterial wipes and hand sanitiser. If in a malarial zone, make sure you avoid getting bitten regardless of your choice of prophylaxis. Use a deterrent and cover your ankles and feet at dusk when mosquitoes are most prevalent.

After a long journey, spend some time going for a brisk walk or doing gentle stretches to unknot yourself. A routine of daily yoga or Pilates will help your body and your mind, too.

69

Don't forget about your mental health

Meditation can release any stresses, and spending time writing,
sketching or colouring can make you feel good. Challenge
yourself, but don't pile on the pressure. If you're tired,
admit it and take a day off. Don't beat yourself up over
anything you haven't done. You're doing well.

70 *And if you do get sick*

Feeling under the weather when you're alone can be particularly miserable and magnify your discomfort. Do let someone else know that you're not feeling well – a member of staff at your hotel, for example. It's reassuring to know that someone else has their eye on you, and you'd be surprised by how many people are eager to help a traveller in need.

If you're in shared accommodation, especially if sleeping in a dorm, you should probably splurge on a private room instead. Be extra careful with yourself and take things really easy. Whatever you do, avoid any unnecessary travel. Make sure you are drinking plenty of liquids and having enough rest. Ask at your accommodation about doctors or pharmacies if needed. You might also want to let someone at home know, not least so they can give you a boost by checking back in on you.

Make sure your travel insurance is up-to-date before you go – one less thing to worry about, and you never know when you might need it.

Homesickness

The first thing to note is that homesickness is normal. Yes, normal! No matter how cool, confident and sorted a fellow traveller may seem on the outside, chances are they have felt homesick at some point. And it can sometimes coincide with not feeling so great physically, or when you're staying somewhere grotty.

- Treat yourself – whether that's eating a big bar of chocolate, booking yourself into a spa for an indulgent treatment, or splurging on a night staying somewhere very special. Pick whatever it is that will give you a lift.

- Exercise. We all know that endorphins lift our mood, so this is the time to go for a hike, a speedwalk or a run. Is there anything you can do with others, such as join an exercise class? Your hotel or hostel may even run classes or can suggest somewhere that does. Otherwise, do yoga, Pilates or a workout in your room. Or put on some lively music you like and dance like no one's watching.

- Join a stimulating group activity. See our tips elsewhere on local tours and local connections.

*Being harassed or **followed***

Harassment can take many forms. Being hissed or sworn at; wolf whistles and catcalls. Pushy street-sellers who won't take no for an answer. Racially or sexually abusive language. It can happen to you regardless of your age or gender.

If someone is making a nuisance of themselves, try to be calm but firm in telling them to leave you alone. If that is not working and you cannot shake them off, getting loud and indignant can be the answer. Call them out and you may well find passers-by coming to your aid. If this is happening often, try to learn the appropriate local phrase to tell them to leave you alone.

Think you're being followed? Cross the street and try to find a group of people you can join or talk to, for example in a café or shop. Or stop in front of a shop window for a while and see if they head off. Either that, or head to a reliable-looking hotel to relax in the lobby for a while. This is always a good way to get your equilibrium back. If they're still hanging around outside, ask the staff for help to move them on, or to call you a taxi. Jewellery shops are also a good refuge and generally have CCTV.

73

*Avoiding **unwanted** sexual advances*

Solo travellers can find themselves unpleasantly targeted in some destinations, especially young women. Do consider the local culture and how they dress. If it's a very conservative society, you may receive unwanted attention if you walk around in shorts, miniskirts or a revealing top. What is considered inappropriate can vary, too – showing your shoulders in some places such as churches, temples or places of worship may be considered inappropriate. Cover up when needed to reduce the hassle.

Wearing a wedding ring can work and having a photo of an imaginary partner on your phone may help.

On public transport, try to avoid situations where someone can push themselves up against you. Sit or stand next to people with whom you feel safe if possible. Avoid alleyways, deserted streets and anywhere you might be at risk on your own.

Sex tourism

Some destinations have become centres of sex tourism, whether
for men or women, and this can lead to misunderstandings. As
ever, stay calm and confident, and try and avoid anywhere
that may be a hotspot, especially at night.
Tourists may be suspicious of you too.

Don't be a target

Avoid displaying obvious signs of wealth such as cameras, expensive jewellery (best left at home anyway) and watches (ditto). Keep the bulk of your money in a money belt under your clothes, but make sure you don't have to access it in public.

The best way to do this is to have a small wallet or purse to hand with only what you need for the day – if you find you need more, you can always go into a bathroom and move some around. Ensure any card you use is in a secure spot on your person where it can't be pickpocketed.

Blending in

Even if you are not worried about inappropriate attention or inadvertently causing offence, it could be that you feel happier, safer or more confident if you are not sticking out quite so obviously as a tourist. It also gives you a deeper immersion into the local culture.

How do people dress locally? If they are smart dressers, you are going to look very out of place if scruffy. Do local people wear vest tops, short sleeves or shorts? You may actually feel uncomfortable if you are dressed very differently.

At home, would you go into your local supermarket or café in a bikini? If the answer is no, ask yourself whether it is appropriate to do so where you are, and slip on a cover-up.

Watch how and where people walk. In the souks of Marrakech, for example, the unwritten local rule is to walk on the right. Modulate your voice, too; no one wants to be the crass tourist who shouts and never listens.

Invest in a local shopping bag, such as a branded supermarket one. In a café or bar, watch what the locals are drinking and order the same. Buy the local newspaper – they're inevitably fascinating and give an insight into your destination and its people. Reading it in a café will really make you feel like a local.

Standing _out_

There are times when you actually may want to stand out a bit. Some solo travellers find that it is a good way to attract other people to them because it gives an opener for conversation. So, wearing a T-shirt with an interesting message on it, having an unusual bag, or having a particularly distinctive hat or scarf can do the trick.

Openly carrying or reading a physical book or a magazine, rather than an electronic device, can have the same effect.

78
*Act **confident** (even when you're not)*

This may seem unfair, but if you act and look anxious or scared, you are probably increasing your chances of a negative encounter. To predators, you could unfortunately look like a victim. So, hold your head high, throw your shoulders back and act confident. Walk with a sense of purpose and as if you know where you are going even if you don't. Make eye contact – as long as it isn't culturally inappropriate. Have a smile ready at your lips, but keep your wits about you. Not only will you look like someone not to mess with, but you will find that you start to feel that way too.

Getting from A to B

Avoid long late-night and overnight bus journeys. They are more prone to accidents and are more likely to be targeted by thieves. Passengers are more likely to have consumed alcohol or to chance their luck with you. Bus stations are to be avoided late at night and preferably the early morning too. Use a seatbelt if the bus has them.

In a taxi, if you are worried about the potential for assault, sit behind the driver, not next to them. Try and have your luggage in with you, rather than the boot. If you feel the driver is going too fast, never be afraid to ask them to slow down.

Car share can be a useful way of getting around and sharing expenses. So, if hiring a car yourself, see if anyone you trust at your accommodation is looking to go in your direction. Or listen out and ask around if staying somewhere on a popular route.

When hiring a car, always check it over meticulously before driving it away, and note every tiny scratch. If you have any sort of accident, do let the car hire company know immediately. One of the joys of having your own wheels is that you really can follow your nose and take any detour you fancy. You can also pick up locals as well as take fellow travellers, but only if you feel safe doing so. Make sure you know local rules and regulations and if driving at night is safe.

Always use the seatbelt. You would wear one at home, so don't act any differently overseas. They really do save lives.

Use your common sense if hiring a motorbike or moped too – they are responsible for a high number of accidents. Always wear a helmet, even if you don't look cool!

80 *If things go wrong*

If you are a victim of crime, report it to the police as soon as you can. If they can't speak English, try to request they can get hold of someone who can, or whether there is another station you can go to. You will need a copy of the police report and a reference number to claim from your insurance company. If you have any difficulties with the police, contact your embassy or consulate.

If your credit card is stolen, report it to the issuer as soon as possible on their app or their emergency number (keep this somewhere in your belongings). They will stop it and can usually issue you a new one within a day or two.

If your passport is stolen, report it immediately to your nearest embassy or consulate. You will need a police report. They will issue emergency travel documentation for a fee (which you can claim back off your insurance). Above all, stay calm.

Smile!

Your biggest secret weapon when you travel. Many things may vary around the world, and some cultures are definitely smilier than others. However, research shows that when different cultures get together, smiling becomes a common currency, a non-verbal method of communication understood by everyone.

Can't speak the language? Smile, and people will try to help you. Feeling nervous but don't want to show it? Smiling will mask it and make you look confident. Find yourself at loggerheads with an official? While there are no guarantees, a grateful smile may break them down.

What's more, smiling is good for you. No matter how fed up, jet lagged or tired you are feeling, smiling will lift your mood. It boosts your immune system, reduces stress and makes you happier. Try it!

Chapter 5
DURING
YOUR STAY

Hurrah, you're there and having a wonderful time. But it is easy sometimes to stay in a rut, let your natural shyness take over, or spend too much time in your hotel or hostel.

Not that there's any problem with simply hanging out curled up with a good book if that's what you want. But don't be one of those people who, months and years later, wish that they had made more of the experience when they were there. Use it to create some incredible life memories.

82

Find your feet

You might be full of energy, but it's still worth taking the time to find your feet and tune in to a new destination. Spending time hanging out in a café just people-watching can often help you to acclimatize. Wander through a park, sit in a public square, find a rooftop café to indulge in mint tea. In a city, orientate yourself by taking some sort of organized tour, even a really touristy hop-on, hop-off bus tour.

Feeling hot, tired and frazzled? Then cooling down in the lobby of a five-star hotel can be amazingly restorative, whether or not you have a glass of something while you're there. Churches, galleries and museums can also be oases of calm.

83 *Take a **local** tour or activity*

Many cities have walking tours, some even offer free ones, and these are a useful option for the first 24 hours. Not only will it help you orientate yourself in a strange city, but it can be an opportunity to meet fellow travellers and to get tips, both from them and the guide.

But there has also been an explosion in unique local experiences you can book through sites such as Viator, airbnb, GetYourGuide, Urban Adventures and Tripadvisor. Heading to Tokyo? Why not visit a sumo stable to see the wrestlers train or join a go-kart convoy through the streets dressed as a comic book character? Staying in Porto? Why not join a tile workshop or a tour of a port house? Learn how to put on and wear a kimono in Kyoto or prepare tacos in a Mexico City home. The world really is your oyster… talking of which, there are even tours where you can learn to shuck the tasty bivalves.

84

*Get to **know** the local scene*

Use travel communities to make contact with locals or other visitors. There are a pack of apps suitable for solo travellers. SoloTraveller connects you with others to find travel companions, share experiences and exchange tips and ideas. Another useful one is Meetup – although aimed at locals rather than visitors, it has proven to be a great way to experience the local scene somewhere. It highlights activities and events by local groups such as running clubs, choirs or photography clubs, bringing together people with shared interests.

Some tourist boards have schemes to connect you with local residents. West Sweden, for instance, has introduced a Meet the Locals scheme, enabling you to go crab fishing or learn about railways with people from the area. Check around other destinations for similar schemes.

The Global Greeter Network connects you to volunteers who can show you around their hometown, while the Showaround site offers a similar service but with a smaller range of destinations and a mix of free and paid guides.

Be open to new experiences, ideas and people. But always trust your instincts. Pick up local papers or newsletters to find details of events and groups. There are often local walking groups, for instance – a great way of finding hidden places.

85 *Walk as **much** as you can*

Not only is walking good for you, but you'll notice more details than you would on public transport, and you really get the feeling of a place to a much greater degree. Use the GPS on your phone to guide you, but also don't be afraid to get lost every now and then (as long as you are not somewhere unsafe).

Alternatively, hire or borrow a bicycle if you can. Many cities around the world now have free bikes, and an increasing number of hostels and guesthouses have them available for guests too.

86 *Put* back

Whether or not you have already pre-booked a volunteer holiday, you may find opportunities to help charities and communities as you travel. Hostels, for instance, sometimes have details of small local organizations that welcome overseas visitors giving a hand. This could be doing anything from playing with puppies at an animal shelter to participating in conversation classes in your native language.

If the idea of spending time on a farm appeals, WWOOF (World Wide Opportunities on Organic Farms) is a network linking volunteers with organic farmers and growers. Essentially, you receive accommodation and food in return for helping with daily tasks.

International Barter Week is a relatively new initiative that takes place each November. The premise is that hotels and B&Bs offer free accommodation in exchange for a skill or service.

Another way to put back is to help out on organized litter pick-ups. Trash Hero is an initiative that started in Thailand to clean the beaches, but it has now spread around the world, and travellers are very welcome. Plogging is a combination of running and picking up litter; it started in Sweden and there are now groups in a growing number of countries.

87
*Don't be embarrassed to be **alone***

If you stay somewhere popular with other overseas travellers, you will meet other people like yourself who are travelling in the same direction. You may therefore make friends with a potential travel buddy, but never feel obliged to travel on with the first person you meet. This is your journey. Decide where you want to go and what you want to do and don't feel pressured to change your plans for others.

Likewise, don't feel you have to hang out with people if you don't feel like it. After all, you likely went away on your own to avoid the pressure of fitting in with others. Just make an excuse or even be honest and say you want some "me time".

88 *Listen to locals*

Please don't be one of those travellers who only hangs out with fellow travellers and doesn't take the opportunity to get to know the locals. Not only is local knowledge incredibly useful, but you'll probably find when you get back home that it is the locals who you remember.

Unfortunately, not every local will have good intentions, so if anyone seems to be latching onto you and too eager to befriend you, then keep your guard up. Fortunately, the bad 'uns will be in the minority.

Of course, not every interaction with a local will be meaningful, but be open to making eye contact and initiating small talk. Just talking to people at the hotel, in shops and in cafés will enhance your experience overall. You are likely to be accepted as someone worth talking to if you regularly visit the same café or restaurant, for instance.

Find out about their lives and their opinions. As the legendary travel writer Paul Theroux says, "Become a stranger in a strange land... Listen to what people are saying."

89 *Try the **lingo***

Speaking the local language to at least a passable level is a huge boon and opens many doors. Not only is it useful on a practical level, but you'll be able to engage and get into conversation with a much wider range of people.

But if you don't know the language, try to have a go at commonly spoken words and phrases. Learn standard greetings and manners such as "please" and "thank you", as well as phrases that will raise awareness to those around you, including "go away" and "help".

Draw up a list of words that may prove useful for day-to-day practicalities, and memorize them. For instance, these could be the words for "bus", "train", "where?", "tomorrow". Have a language app such as Duolingo downloaded on your phone.

It's handy and enjoyable to have swotted up on menu choices. If you have dietary restrictions, learn the relevant phrases for those and how to describe them if necessary. For example, you may need to list what you do not eat but also suggest what you *can* eat.

Never be afraid to ask what something means or how to say something in the local lingo. It can be a great icebreaker, and people generally love you attempting their language.

90 *Talk to other travellers*

Part of the joy of travel can also be meeting other travellers. Don't always wait for other people to make the first move – they may be shy, feel awkward or feel tired. So, smile, introduce yourself, and show interest in other people too. Find out where they have been and where they are going next. Ask for recommendations and share yours.

If heading out of your accommodation for a meal or drink, see if anyone wants to go with you. Chat to other people who are clearly on their own in restaurants, bars and cafés; you can always see if they want to join your table.

Of course, not everyone will want to be your friend, so don't take it badly if rebuffed. Maybe they're just having a bad day.

Help other travellers

You might sometimes feel shy, awkward or out of sorts,
and it's easy to think it's just you having those emotions. But
other travellers will be going through everything you are – and
possibly more. So, lend a hand to any travellers, especially
solo ones, who may be feeling homesick, poorly or just tired.
Pay it forward.

Dating

The romance of the road is a well-known phrase. But, romance on the road is talked about less often. Yet meeting someone romantically when travelling offers an extra frisson and can be a very intense experience. Whether locals or fellow travellers, the world seems full of much more interesting strangers than when we are at home.

Part of the joy of travelling is that you can experiment and hook up with someone very different to who you would at home. And you can put on a different persona too.

Whatever you do, use the same common-sense rules you would at home. In these days of social media, you could see what platforms they are on, and get a feel for them and their friends. Let someone, whether at home or where you are staying, know who you are going on a date with, including their social media profiles, and ideally where. Meet in the daytime first, and in a neutral and busy public place.

Don't send out mixed or misleading messages. Be clear about whether you are just looking for a bit of companionship (e.g. someone to have dinner with), a fun flirtation, a raunchy time or indeed something potentially more serious.

And be honest when saying goodbye too. It has been known for smitten former lovers to turn up on the other's doorstep… "Surprise!"

 *Buy **local***

While it's tempting to take everything you need on a trip, you'll not only be weighing yourself down unnecessarily, you'll be depriving yourself of one of life's great pleasures by not shopping as you go along.

And don't just visit the city department store. They're worth a visit just out of interest – how do they compare with the ones you visit back home? – but seek out independent shops instead:

- You won't need to take as much with you in the first place

- You'll have more meaningful interactions with locals

- You'll be spreading your money out around communities

- You'll get a better, deeper understanding of local culture

- You'll feel more immersed

94
Use local **services**

It can be easy to deprive yourself of things that need doing, or to get them done at the soulless international city hotel where you find yourself spending a night. Whether you need a haircut, leg wax, zip repaired or your shoes shined, find it locally. You'll be spreading money among those who need it. You may find a really talented craftsperson. You'll be talking to people who aren't in tourism. You'll probably have fun. And you may even have an experience that you'll be able to talk about for years to come.

Travel the ***beaten*** *path*

Independent travellers tend to follow well-worn paths, particularly in Asia, Australia and New Zealand. The advantage of this if you are a first time solo traveller is that there is plentiful accommodation en route, a decent transport network, and lots of advice and information along the way.

You'll also get to meet plenty of fellow travellers, if you want. You can still go as slow or as fast as you want and take any diversions as you go along.

Head off the beaten path

If you're feeling more confident or really want to push yourself, it is surprisingly easy to get off the beaten track. Just follow your nose along the quieter byways, ask locally for recommendations and ideas, and be as flexible as possible in your thinking.

Do let people know where you are going each day if possible. There may be someone back home you keep updated. If you get lost or stranded, run out of petrol, or have any other kind of problem, help is more likely to come if people know (a) that you're missing, and (b) where to start the search. If in doubt, check out the safety tips in Chapter 4 (pages 74–97).

97 *Say yes **more***

It's always easier to say no to something than to say yes. You can always find a reason not to have a go at something scary. But, here you are, with a host of new experiences you can try so step out of your comfort zone. Who's going to care if you fall off the paddle board, if you're rubbish at yoga, if you get out of breath climbing the peak? It's overcoming the things that worry or scare us the most that give us the greatest sense of achievement.

They say that when you look back on your life you only regret what you *didn't* do. Don't be that person. Say yes.

98

Don't forget about "you"

If the point of going away was to get some "me time", make
sure you get it. There is nothing wrong with enjoying a good
book, completely chilling, or being selfish in what you do. Don't
put yourself under self-inflicted pressure. Don't think about
deadlines. Don't think you have to tick off a list of things
to see and do. If you usually lead a busy life, then
being alone can be rejuvenating and energizing.
Embrace solitude. Your mind and body will
thank you for it.

99

*Don't be a **slave** to your camera – but do take photographs*

Whatever you do, don't live on your phone or spend all your time behind a camera. And don't get obsessed with finding the perfect Instagram shot. If you do, you risk not really seeing or experiencing all that is interesting.

But do take some photos as you go along to record your trip; just be selective about what you shoot. Don't bother with endless photos of the view or wildlife shots where the animal is so far away that you can't make it out. Instead, capture the people you meet, the experiences you have, the food, and the quirky little details that you will have forgotten afterwards.

*Keep a blog or **journal***

Whether you are away for a year, a month, a week or a weekend, your trip has been a journey in more ways than one. This applies even more so when you have travelled solo, as you will have enjoyed experiences that may have eluded you otherwise.

So keep a record of it all – of what you did and how you did it. You may also want to capture how you felt and who you met. Then choose where to record it. You might simply want to capture it all on social media, and there is nothing wrong with that. But this is your chance to create a more permanent record that you can look back on in years to come.

Maybe keep a blog, whether for friends and family to view, or to share your experiences and recommendations with the wider world. You may even find a new hobby or career doing so. Many professional bloggers and travel writers started off being inspired on a solo trip.

Or you could keep a more personal and physical journal. There is something very therapeutic and inspiring about keeping a diary, and you can keep your thoughts private. And it doesn't just have to be your scribbles – you can add in sketches, stick in tickets, write scraps of poetry.

FINALLY

*Live in the **moment***

You've come all this way, so live every minute of it. Don't sit round with headphones on, isolating yourself from the place you are in. Don't constantly contact home to see how everyone is. When you meet other travellers, don't spend all your time talking about your life and career back home. And definitely don't be the travel bore who talks about the places they have been, the other trips they have done.

This is your opportunity to have one of the best experiences of your life. One that will feed you a lifetime of memories. So, live it.

Resources

FURTHER READING

The Grand Hostels: Luxury Hostels of the World by BudgetTraveller (Kash Bhattacharya).

The Travel Survival Guide by Lloyd Figgins.

Wanderlust magazine. Available in print or digital editions, the magazine has a high proportion of solo traveller readers. Inspiration and information on destinations around the world and advice on how to travel well.

WWOOF (World Wide Opportunities on Organic Farms) connects volunteers with organic farmers who offer bed and board in exchange for help.

BLOGS AND WEBSITES

Wanderlust Visit the Wanderlust website to see a curated list of the best solo travel articles. https://www.wanderlust.co.uk/interests/solo-travel/

Girlsthattravel.com Gemma Thompson is passionate about solo female travel and her site features a great mix of practical advice and inspiration.

Eatwith.com offer supper clubs, dinner parties, cooking classes and other opportunities to eat with locals.

Travelingspoon.com another great site for connecting food-loving travellers to local hosts.

Global Greeter Network connects you to volunteers who want to share their hometown with you. https://globalgreeternetwork.info/

The International Greeter Association is a network of locals offering free walking tours of where they live. https://internationalgreeter.org/

Showaround is a service connecting travellers to local guides - some offer free tours while others charge. https://www.showaround.com/

Urban Adventures contains an interesting range of day tours with local guides. https://www.urbanadventures.com/

Foreign, Commonwealth & Development Office travel advice (FCDO) gives travel advice by country regarding terrorism, natural disasters and other safety matters. https://www.gov.uk/foreign-travel-advice

APPS

SoloTraveller connects you with others to find travel companions, share experiences and exchange tips and ideas.

Meetup – although aimed at locals rather than visitors, it has proved to be a great way to experience the local scene somewhere as it brings together people with shared interests (e.g. running clubs, choirs, photography clubs) and highlights, activities and events.

PODCASTS

A Girl's Guide to Travelling Alone Likeable host Gemma Thompson specialises in solo travel and each episode focuses on a different aspect, whether practical info or a touch of inspiration.

My Solo Road Have you been tempted by the thought of an extended trip by campervan? Californian Sydney Ferbache gives an insight into her #VanLife as a solo female. She tackles everything from safety, finances and loneliness to her own experiences.

Solo Travel with Victoria Rose Just to prove that you can travel solo at any age Victoria Rose is a 69-year-old Australian who loves to share her tips and tales of travelling on a pension.

Index

0.6l fill&go Active
    bottle 74
accommodation 56
Africa, East 44
age 6
airbnb 101
airport lounges 48
alone, being 19, 105
Andalusian horses 24
Antarctic, the 41
anti-bacterial wipes 84
appreciation of home
    27
Arctic, the 41
Argentina 10, 24
arrival 78
art holidays 43
Asia, South-East 33
attack alarm 83
Australia 33
avoiding
    harassment 88
    late-night journeys
    95
    sexual advances 89

backpack 49
Bangkok 62
barge cruise 41

beaten path, the 113,
    114
being alone 19, 105
bespoke trips 33, 45
Bhattacharya, Kash 58
bicycles 41, 103
bird-watching 43
blending in 92
blog 118
books 53
boredom 52
brave 6
Brazil 24
BRITA 74
bubble 16
budget 7
budgeting for the
    unexpected 22
buffets 71
buying local 111

cafés 69
Camargue horses 24
camera 52–3
cameras 91
campervans 63
camps 42
Canada 33
Cape Town 44

car hire company 95
car sharing 95
cards 91
career break 21
cash 91
challenge yourself 40
challenges, unexpected
    28
changing your life 29
charities 40
Chiang Mai 10, 62
clothing layers 50
colouring book 52
comfortable on your
    own 19
communal areas 60
companies are bonded
    45
compromise 10
confidence 6, 29, 94
cookery holidays 43
cooking parties 75
cotton 50
Couchsurfing 57
credit card theft 96
crime, victim of 96
Croatia 41
cruising 41
Cuba 24

CV 21
cycling 40, 41
Cyprus 46

dancing 24
dating 110
dealing with boredom 52
decisions 18
diary 118
dining with others 67
dinner parties 75
dinner seating 68
do what you want 10
doctors 86
don't be a target 91
dormitories 59
drivers 22, 45
Duolingo app 107

ear plugs 59
eating experiences 75
eating right 69
eatwith.com 75
eco-friendly wash 51
Ecofiltro 74
Ecuador 35
emotional baggage 15
endorphins 40
enjoying magnificent
    views 23
Everest Base Camp 40
exercising 84, 87
Exodus Travels 41
expedition cruises 41

expeditions 44
eye mask 59

feeling your senses 23
felucca 41
Figgins, Lloyd 83
finding your feet 100
first aid essentials 51
first nights 78, 79
fleece 50
flexibility 17
following a passion 24
following a quest 24
food courts 72
foodie walking tours 75
foodies 24
France 24
freedom, sense of 7
friends 10, 12
Friendship Travel 46

Galápagos Islands 35
germs 84
GetYourGuide 101
Global Greeter
    Network 102
going your own pace
    20
*Grand Hostels, The:
    Luxury Hostels of the
    World* 58
GRAYL GEOPRESS 74
Great Wall of China
    40

Greek islands 41
group activity 87
group travel 36, 37
    38, 45, 67
Guatemala 74
guides 45, 102
gulet 41

hand sanitiser 84
harassment, avoiding 88
hat 51
headlamp 51
headspace 15
helmets 95
helping 109
Holiday Extras 48
home, appreciation
    of 27
homesickness 87
homestay 57
honeymoon couples 42
horse-riding 43
horses 24
hostels 58
hydration 84

independent travel 35,
    36, 45
insurance 86, 96
interests 24,
International Barter
    Week 104

jacket 50

journal 52, 118
juggling lives 15
Just You 46

keeping in touch 80
Kerala backwaters 41
Kilimanjaro 40
Kindle 53
Kyoto 101

language 107
language holidays 43
late-night journeys,
   avoiding 95
Latin America 24
layers of clothing 50
learning holiday 43
life changing 29
light packing 49
Lippizaner horses 24
listening to nature 23
live in the moment 16,
   119
local activities 101
local adventures 11
local buying 111
local services 112
locals 106
lockers 59
lodges 42
LoungeBuddy 48
luggage 77, 81
lunch 66

make your own
   decisions 18
makeup 51
making time 70
Malaysia 36
man-made fabrics 50
markets, street 72
Marrakech 10, 92
"me time" 116
meaningful experience
   25
meditation 85
Meet the Locals 102
meeting people 12
Meetup 102
mental health 85
Menu del Dia 66
merino wool 50
Mexico City 101
microfibre towel 51
money belt 50, 59, 91
moped hire 95
mosquitoes 84
motorbike hire 95
motorhomes 63

Nakd raisins 73
natural fabrics 50
Nepalese Himalayas
   46
Netherlands, the 41
new experiences 29,
   115
New Zealand 33

newspapers, local 92
Nile, river 41
No1 Lounges 48
nuts 73

offers 38, 39
other travellers 108,
   109
overlanding 44
oyster shucking 101

pace 20
packing light 49
partner 10
passport theft 96
patatas bravas 24
personal growth 28
personas 14
pharmacies 86
phone power bank 51
photography 52–3,
   117
photography holidays
   43
playing cards 52
Plogging 104
polar cruise 41
police 96
popcorn 73
Porto 101
power bank, phone 51
pre-booking
   accommodation 79
Priority Pass 48

private journeys 45
PROPER popcorn 73
purse 91

quietness 23

rafting 40
reading 53
restaurants 69
right destination, the 33
right time to go 34
right trip, the 32
river cruises 41
romance of the road 110
romantic hotels 61
room locks 64
room safety 64
room security 64
room service 65
rooms 64
Round the World ticket 35
rucksack 49
Russian meal 75

safaris 42
safety 79, 83
sailing 41
St Petersburg 75
salsa 24
samba 24
sandals, waterproof 50
saving money 22

say yes 115
scamming 82
scarf 51
seasons 34
seatbelts 95
seating places 70
seaweed, dried 73
self-care 84
self-confidence 11
self-discovery 13
sense of freedom 7
serendipity 26
sex tourism 90
sexual advances, avoiding 89
sharing rooms 38
shoes 50
Showaround 102
sickness 86
silk 50
Singapore 33, 36
single 6
single supplements 38, 39
sketch pad 52
skills for CV 21
sleeper trains 62
Slovenia 24
smiling 97
snacks 73
sobriety 83
solitude 116
solo specialist tour companies 46

solo-only departures 39
Solos Holidays 46
SoloTraveller 102
Spain 24
special interest holidays 43
specialist tour companies 46
splurging money 22
spontaneity 17
standing out 93
staying sober 83
stomach issues 71
strangers 12
street markets 72
stretching 84
style 7
suitcase, wheelie 49
sun protection 51
supper clubs 75
supplement-free holidays 39
Sweden 104
Sweden, west 102

tailormade travel 45
talking 108
Tangier 44
tango 24
target, don't be one 91
taxis 95
Thailand 33, 36, 47, 62, 104
Theroux, Paul 106

time, making 70
toiletries 51
toilets 81, 84
Tokyo 101
torch 51
tour leader 36, 38
towel, microfibre 51
trainers, black 50
trains, sleeper 62
Trash Hero 104
travel advisories 33
travel agents 45
travel communities 102
travel insurance 86
Travel One 46
Travel Survival Guide, The: Get Smart, Stay Safe 83
travelingspoon.com 75
travelling light 49
treating yourself 87
trekking 40
Tripadvisor 101
truck expeditions 44
Tuscany 46

unexpected challenges 28
United States 24, 33
unlicensed taxis 83
Urban Adventures 101

valuables security 81
Viator 101

Vietnam 33
vitamin tablets 84
Voluntary Service Overseas 47
volunteer holiday 104
volunteering 47
VSO 47
vulnerability 78, 80, 81, 82

walking 103
walking away 82
walking tours 101
wallet 91
wash, eco-friendly 51
watches 91
water bottle 51
water filters 74
water purifiers 74
Water-to-Go 74
whale watching 24
what do you want 32
wheelie suitcase 49
where to stay 56
wildlife trips 42
World Wide Opportunities on Organic Farms 104

yoga holidays 43

zip pockets 50